AIR

Written by Alex Hall

ELEMENTS

Gareth Stevens
PUBLISHING

Please visit our website, www.garethstevens.com. For a free color catalog of all our high-quality books, call toll free 1-800-542-2595 or fax 1-877-542-2596.

Published in 2025 by
Gareth Stevens Publishing
2544 Clinton St.
Buffalo, NY 14224

Written by:
Alex Hall

Edited by:
Rebecca Phillips-Bartlett

Designed by:
Ker Ker Lee

Cataloging-in-Publication Data

Names: Hall, Alex.
Title: Air / Alex Hall.
Description: Buffalo, NY : Gareth Stevens Publishing, 2025. | Series: Elements | Includes glossary and index.
Identifiers: ISBN 9781482468519 (pbk.) | ISBN 9781482468526 (library bound) | ISBN 9781482468533 (ebook)
Subjects: LCSH: Air--Juvenile literature. | Four elements (Philosophy)--Juvenile literature.
Classification: LCC QC161.2 H355 2025 | DDC 551.5--dc23

This edition is published by arrangement with Booklife Publishing

Printed in the United States of America

CPSIA compliance information: Batch #CW25GS: For further information contact Gareth Stevens at 1-800-542-2595.

Find us on

Photo Credits – Images are courtesy of Shutterstock.com, with thanks to Getty Images, Thinkstock Photo, and iStockphoto.

Recurring images – gravity_point. Cover – 4045, Valentina Shilkina, Nature Peaceful. 2–3 – happycreator. 4–5 – Studio Light and Shade, alb2018. 6–7 – alb2018, Santhosh Varghese. 8–9 – Brian A Jackson, Dustie. 10–11 – Sunny studio, Greg Brave. 12–13 – Todd Shoemake, Benjamin Simeneta. 14–15 – Lukas Jonaitis, Sari ONeal. 16–17 – nEwyyy, Kodda, LeManna. 18–19 – fokke baarssen, WINDCOLORS. 20–21 – Evgeny Atamanenko, savitskaya iryna, Igor Kovalenko. 22–23 – Hakase_420, Mikadun.

CONTENTS

Words that look like <u>this</u> can be found in the glossary on page 24.

ESSENTIAL ELEMENTS

The four elements are water, earth, fire, and air. Life on our planet would not be possible without them. Each element has its own important job. These elements are so important that they are known as the essential elements.

Air is all around us. Air is one of the main things that makes life on our planet possible. We use air for important things, but we also use it for fun things too.

The facts about air will blow you away!

WHAT IS AIR?

Air is made of a mix of gases. Most gases are invisible. They spread out to fill any space available. As the gases spread, they mix to create air.

The main gases in the air are called oxygen and nitrogen. Oxygen is a gas that most living things need to live. Most of the air is made of nitrogen. Nitrogen is needed for plants to grow.

Other gases, such as carbon dioxide, are also in air.

WINDY WEATHER

Wind is caused by changes in the temperature of air, land, and water. If air flows over warm things, the air heats up and rises. This creates space for colder air to flow, creating wind.

Changes in air pressure can make wind faster. This is why some winds are stronger than others. Some wind is strong enough to damage, or harm, what's in its path.

Changes in air pressure are why the weather changes.

TAKE A BREATH

Breathe in. Breathe out. Breathing is something that we do all the time without thinking. Air is needed to keep our bodies working. Almost all animals need air to breathe and stay alive.

Many plants need carbon dioxide and oxygen from the air to stay alive. Green plants use sunlight to turn carbon dioxide into oxygen. This gives plants energy.

TORNADOES

Tornadoes are natural disasters. Natural disasters are events that are not caused by humans. Tornadoes are tubes of air that stretch from the clouds down to the ground.

Tornado winds can go faster than a race car.

Tornadoes are caused by wind from large thunderstorms moving at different speeds and directions. This causes the wind to rotate. The rotating wind moves so fast it reaches the ground.

Tornadoes are powerful enough to knock down buildings.

TAKE COVER!

THERE ARE A FEW SIGNS THAT A TORNADO IS ON THE WAY. LOOK OUT FOR THESE THINGS:

- A dark or green sky
- Large dark, low clouds
- A loud roar from the sky

WHAT TO DO IN A TORNADO:

- Go somewhere underground such as a basement.
- Stay away from windows.
- Hide under something strong such as a desk.
- Cover your body with something soft.

AIR POLLUTION

Many harmful gases are put into the air by humans. These gases are created by things such as factories, some cars, and airplanes. These gases cause pollution. Pollution is bad because it harms the environment.

Smog is smoke and fog caused by air pollution.

There are ways to help lower air pollution. Biking or walking to school instead of using a car reduces, or lowers, how much pollution is put into the air.

We all need to work together to reduce air pollution.

THE POWER OF WIND

Humans use electricity every day. Some ways of making electricity create air pollution. However, wind can be used to create electricity without harming the planet. Wind turbines are one way of making electricity from wind.

A group of wind turbines is called a wind farm.

Wind turbines are used to collect strong winds high in the sky. The wind blows the blades of the wind turbine. The movement of the blades is turned into electricity.

FUN IN THE AIR

There are many fun activities that use the air. Have you ever tried flying a kite? Kites use the wind to stay high in the air.

Birds use the air to fly. Some people go bird-watching to watch birds flying and resting in nature. Bird-watching is a quiet and calm activity for people who enjoy the outdoors.

AMAZING AIR

The element of air is needed for most life on our planet. Air has the oxygen we need to breathe. It also has the carbon dioxide that plants need to grow and create more oxygen.

Air is an amazing element for so many reasons. It is all around us even though we cannot see it. Can you think of any other things that use air?

GLOSSARY

air pressure the force that air puts on something

balance the state in which things exist in the correct amounts to keep things stable

carbon dioxide a natural gas that is found in the air that humans breathe out

energy the power that makes living things able to move and live

environment the natural world

invisible unable to be seen

rotate to move in a circle

temperature how hot or cold something is

INDEX